At the Fire Station

By Sophie Geister-Jones

level
2
little blue
readers

www.littlebluehousebooks.com

Little Blue House is distributed by North Star Editions:
sales@northstareditions.com | 888-417-0195

Produced for Little Blue House by Red Line Editorial.

Photographs ©: GaryTalton/iStockphoto, cover; monkeybusinessimages/iStockphoto, 4; DnHolm/iStockphoto, 7 (top); undefined undefined/iStockphoto, 7 (bottom); MSPhotographic/iStockphoto, 9; Matt277/iStockphoto, 10; kali9/iStockphoto, 12–13, 24 (top left); kali9/iStockphoto, 15, 24 (bottom left); AlexSava/iStockphoto, 16; digital94086/iStockphoto, 19, 24 (bottom right); sasacvetkovic33/iStockphoto, 20–21, 24 (top right); Ogen/iStockphoto, 23

Library of Congress Control Number: 2019908617

ISBN
978-1-64619-029-4 (hardcover)
978-1-64619-068-3 (paperback)
978-1-64619-107-9 (ebook pdf)
978-1-64619-146-8 (hosted ebook)

Printed in the United States of America
Mankato, MN
012020

About the Author

Sophie Geister-Jones likes reading, spending time with her family, and eating cheese. She lives in Minnesota.

Table of Contents

At the Fire Station

We go to the fire station.

We meet the firefighters

who work there.

We learn about fires.

We learn about the tools firefighters use.

The tools put out fires.

We see the fire pole.

A firefighter slides down.

It is faster than taking

the stairs.

Fire Clothes

Firefighters wear special clothes. These clothes keep firefighters safe.

Firefighters wear coats.

Firefighters wear pants.

The coats and pants cannot catch on fire.

13

Firefighters wear helmets. Helmets keep their heads safe while they work.

helmet

Fire Trucks

We see the fire trucks.

The fire trucks are big
and red.

They have loud sirens.

The fire truck has a ladder.

The ladder is long.

It helps firefighters put out a fire.

ladder

The fire truck has a hose.

The hose sprays water.

The water puts out fires.

We sit in the fire truck.
We have a fun day at the fire station.

DANGER

THIS VEHICLE HAS
A SEATING CAPACITY
OF 5 PERSONNEL
CARRYING ADDITIONAL
PERSONNEL MAY
RESULT IN

DEATH OR
SERIOUS INJURY

CAUTION !

MUST BE DISCONNECTED !

Glossary

firefighters

hose

helmet

ladder

Index